Clip Art for All Seasons

Finally! The clip art book you have been waiting for! Instructional Fair's **Clip Art for All Seasons** is a 160-page book jam-packed with hundreds of pictures perfect to use for every occasion throughout the year.

Organized month by month, the vast array of exciting seasonal art items contained in this book is perfect for all of your bulletin boards, homework papers, holiday announcements, invitations, learning centers, yearbooks, collages, newsletters and many more topics and projects involved in the teaching profession no matter what time of year. The possibilities are endless!

Also included for each month are calendar headers. These are great when enlarged and used on bulletin boards or with calendars. Other special items found throughout the book include special awards to use to reward students' behavior or work, borders to create your own festive notepaper, and notepaper already put together and ready to use for whatever reasons you may need it.

All art contained within these 160 pages is printed on one side only, so clipping art directly from the book doesn't interfere with anything on the back. Though it may be easier to photocopy what you need so you will have it to use again.

So now you can relax when it comes time to be creative, because with our fantastic clip art book, all the hard work is done! Just clip or copy and enjoy!

Dedication

We at Instructional Fair dedicate this book to all the busy teachers who work so hard to make the school environment a special place to be! We thank you!

Many hours have been spent searching through our products to find art that would brighten your classroom throughout the year. We hope it has been organized in a manner that will give you easy access to what you want, when you want it. Have a great year!

 MARCH

 APRIL

MAY

JUNE

 JULY

 AUGUST

 September

October

 NOVEMBER

DECEMBER

JANUARY

 FEBRUARY

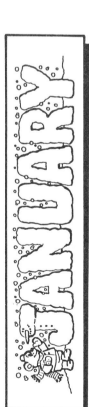

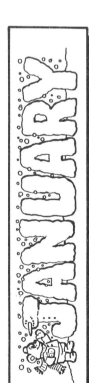

SEPTEMBER

4

5

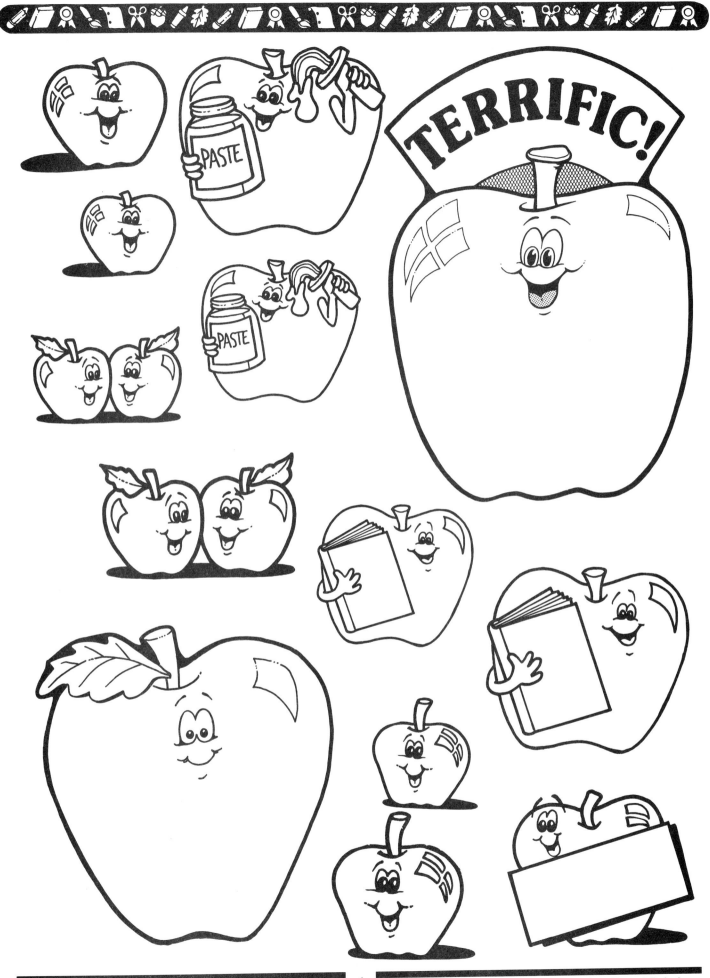

TERRIFIC!

THE
COURTESY
AWARD

is given to

_____

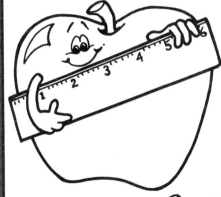

For: _____

Clip Art/Seasons   IF8625

JOHNNY APPLESEED'S BIRTHDAY
September 26th

HAPPY BIRTHDAY JOHNNY!

"BEAR"-Y GOOD!

_____ name

You've _____

Signed _____ Date _____

SUPER READER!

_____ is "DINO"-MITE!

Signed _____

Date _____

Terrific   Terrific

Clip Art/Seasons   IF8625

QUIET,
PLEASE!

QUIET,
PLEASE!

Quiet,
please.

SHHHH!

Quiet,
please.

SHHHH!

12

green

brown

orange

black

green

brown

orange

black

Clip Art/Seasons IF8625

yellow

purple

yellow

purple

blue

red

blue

red

Clip Art/Seasons   IF8625
©MCMXCII Instructional Fair, Inc.

Clip Art/Seasons IF8625

_____ needs to

work on _____

Please help your child
better understand by

_____

_____

_____

Thank you,

_____

_____
Date

MEMO TO:

FROM:

SUBJECT:

DATE: _____

Clip Art/Seasons   IF8625

Clip Art/Seasons IF8625

OCTOBER

Clip Art/Seasons   IF8625

Trick
or
Treat

Clip Art/Seasons   IF8625

Clip Art/Seasons   IF8625

BOO!

Trick or Treat!

Trick or Treat!

29

Clip Art/Seasons IF8625

Clip Art/Seasons   IF8625

Something to HOWL about!

Name _____

Date _____

FANG-TASTIC WORK!

Name _____

Date _____

Clip Art/Seasons   IF8625

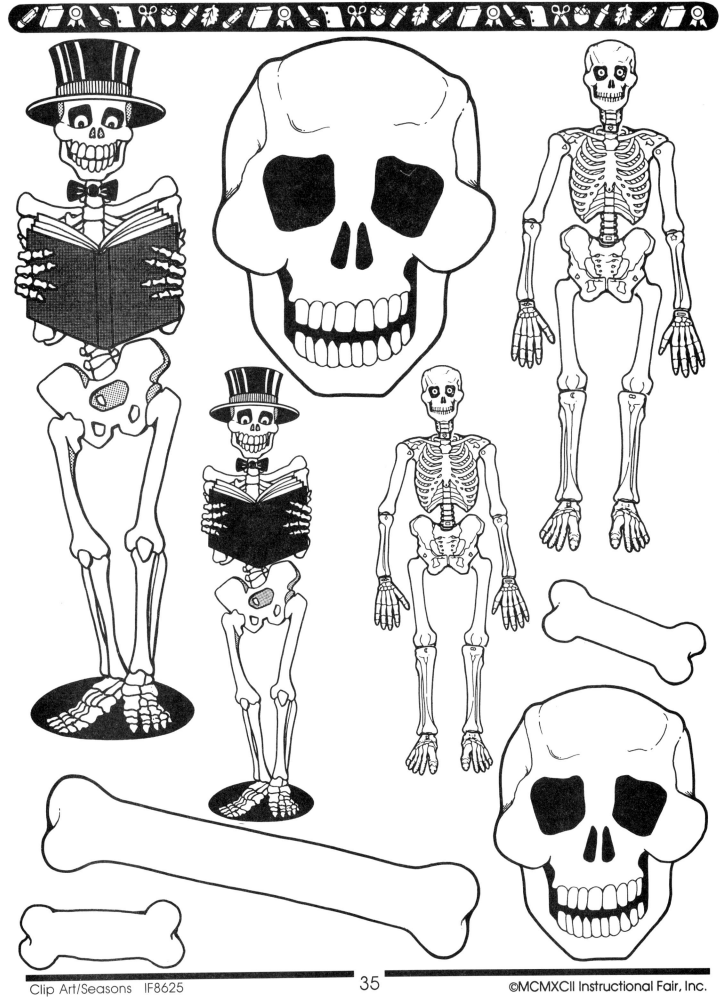

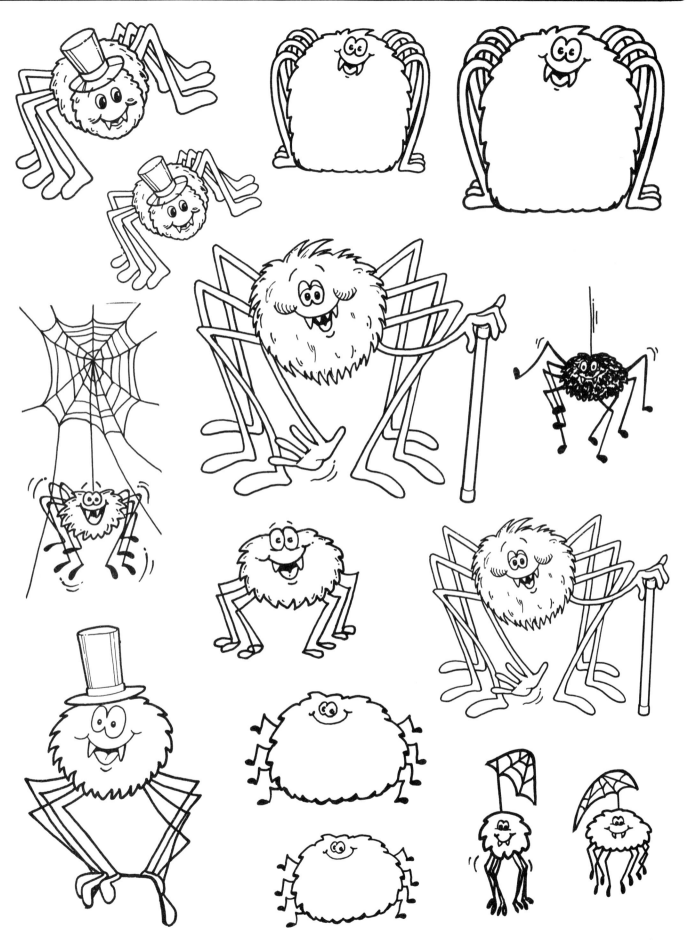

Fire
Prevention

FIRE PREVENTION AWARD

to

_____

Name

_____

for learning how to help prevent fires
and
for promising to follow Fire Safety rules.

_____   _____

TEACHER   DATE

SANTA MARIA

SANTA MARIA

Columbus
Day

NINA

NINA

Clip Art/Seasons   IF8625

Columbus

1492

N

W

E

S

Clip Art/Seasons IF8625

©MCMXCII Instructional Fair, Inc.

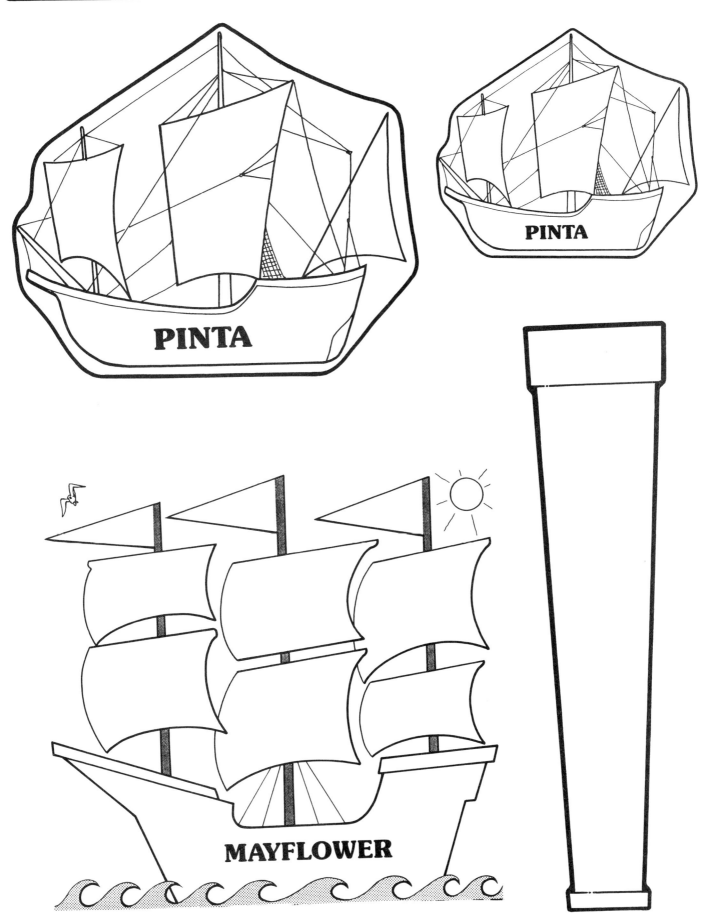

PINTA

PINTA

MAYFLOWER

Clip Art/Seasons   IF8625

Happy
Birthday
Teddy
Roosevelt
October 27

HAPPY BIRTHDAY, TEDDY!

Celebrate Teddy Roosevelt's birthday, October 27th!

Clip Art/Seasons   IF8625

©MCMXCII Instructional Fair, Inc.

NOVEMBER

HAPPY THANKSGIVING

46

Happy
Thanksgiving

has done a

TUR-RIFIC Job!

Clip Art/Seasons   IF8625

49

Clip Art/Seasons   IF8625   ©MCMXCII Instructional Fair, Inc.

©MCMXCII Instructional Fair, Inc.

Election Day!

First Tuesday in November

IF I BECOME PRESIDENT...

VOTE

VOTE

Children's
Book
Week
Third Week
in November

Clip Art/Seasons IF8625

DECEMBER

Clip Art/Seasons IF8625

You Have a Great Gift!

Clip Art/Seasons   IF8625

MERRY CHRISTMAS

HERE COMES SANTA CLAUS!

63

Clip Art/Seasons   IF8625

Bright Things

to

Glow

About!

Name _____ Date _____

Clip Art/Seasons   IF8625

©MCMXCII Instructional Fair, Inc.

Dear Santa,

Your friend,

Clip Art/Seasons IF8625

©MCMXCII Instructional Fair, Inc.

TWELVE DAYS OF CHRISTMAS

DAY 1

DAY 2

DAY 3

DAY 4

DAY 5

DAY 6

DAY 7

DAY 8

DAY 9

DAY 10

DAY 11

DAY 12

BOOM
BOOM
BOOM

Learning's
a
Snap!

Name

Date

FESTIVAL **OF LIGHTS**

HAPPY HANUKKAH!

SPIN THE DREIDEL!!

Clip Art/Seasons IF8625

First Day of Winter

JANUARY

VERY GOOD WORK!

PRESENTED TO

FOR

PRESENTED THIS _____ DAY OF _____ 19 ___

SIGNATURE

Clip Art/Seasons IF8625

©MCMXCII Instructional Fair, Inc.

COOL!

COOL KID AWARD!

Presented to _____
for _____

Signed _____ Date _____

Off to a Great New Year!

Clip Art/Seasons   IF8625

Clip Art/Seasons   IF8625

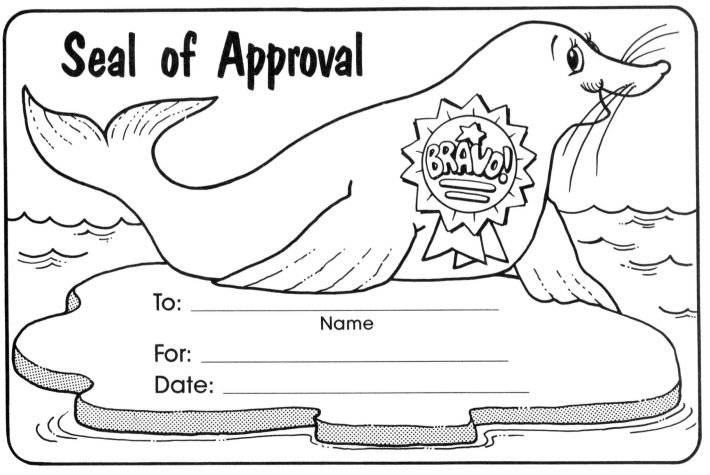

Seal of Approval

To: _____
Name

For: _____

Date: _____

81

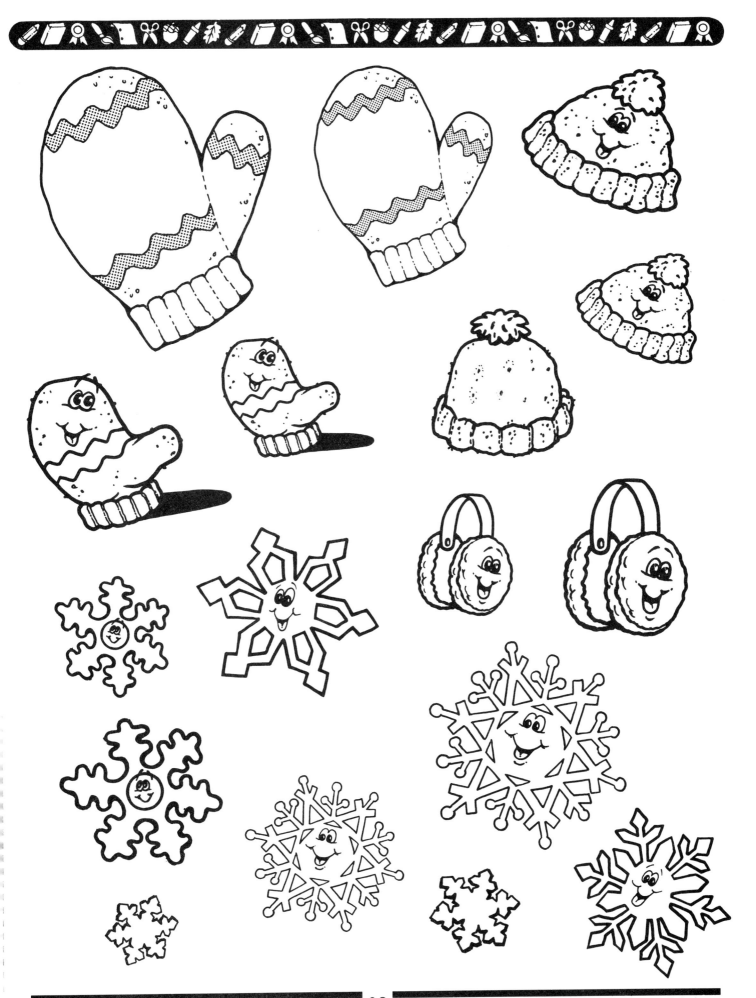

Clip Art/Seasons   IF8625

HAPPY NEW YEAR!

JAN 1

IT'S A NEW YEAR!

CHINESE NEW YEAR

Symbol of Good Luck!

DRAGONS!

You will be very happy!

Clip Art/Seasons   IF8625

MARTIN LUTHER KING, JR. DAY

January 15th

Clip Art/Seasons   IF8625   ©MCMXCII Instructional Fair, Inc.

Happy Birthday, Ben!

Benjamin Franklin's Birthday
January 17th

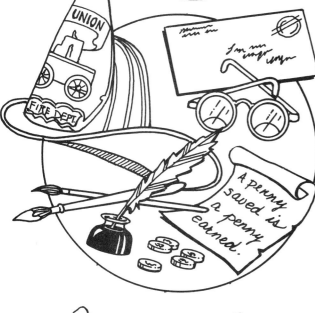

FEBRUARY

Valentine's Day

VALENTINE'S DAY
February 14th

Clip Art/Seasons IF8625
©MCMXCII Instructional Fair, Inc.

You've Really Put Your Heart into Your Work!!

Name:_____

Date:_____

Clip Art/Seasons   IF8625

Clip Art/Seasons   IF8625

©MCMXCII Instructional Fair, Inc.

Clip Art/Seasons   IF8625   ©MCMXCII Instructional Fair, Inc.

BEYOND A SHADOW OF A DOUBT!

You're the Greatest!

Name:_____

Date:_____

GROUNDHOG DAY
February 2nd

FEB. 2

George
Washington's
Birthday

February 22nd

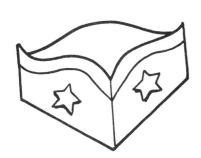

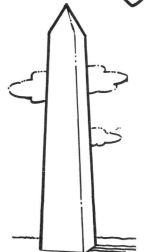

Abraham
Lincoln's
Birthday

February 12th

Abraham Lincoln's
Birthday

Clip Art/Seasons   IF8625

MARCH

ST. PATRICK'S DAY
March 17th

Clip Art/Seasons   IF8625

I'm a Neat Kid!

IRELAND
ULSTER
CONNACHT
LEINSTER
MUNSTER
N

IRELAND
ULSTER
CONNACHT
LEINSTER
MUNSTER
N

Clip Art/Seasons IF8625

©MCMXCII Instructional Fair, Inc.

You're Solid Gold!

Name: _____

Date: _____

Clip Art/Seasons   IF8625

Your Work Has Really Taken Off!

GREAT WORK

Name:_____

Date:_____

Up and Away...

The Sky's the Limit!

March comes in like a lion...

. . . and goes out like a lamb.

Clip Art/Seasons   IF8625

APRIL

HAPPY EASTER

EASTER

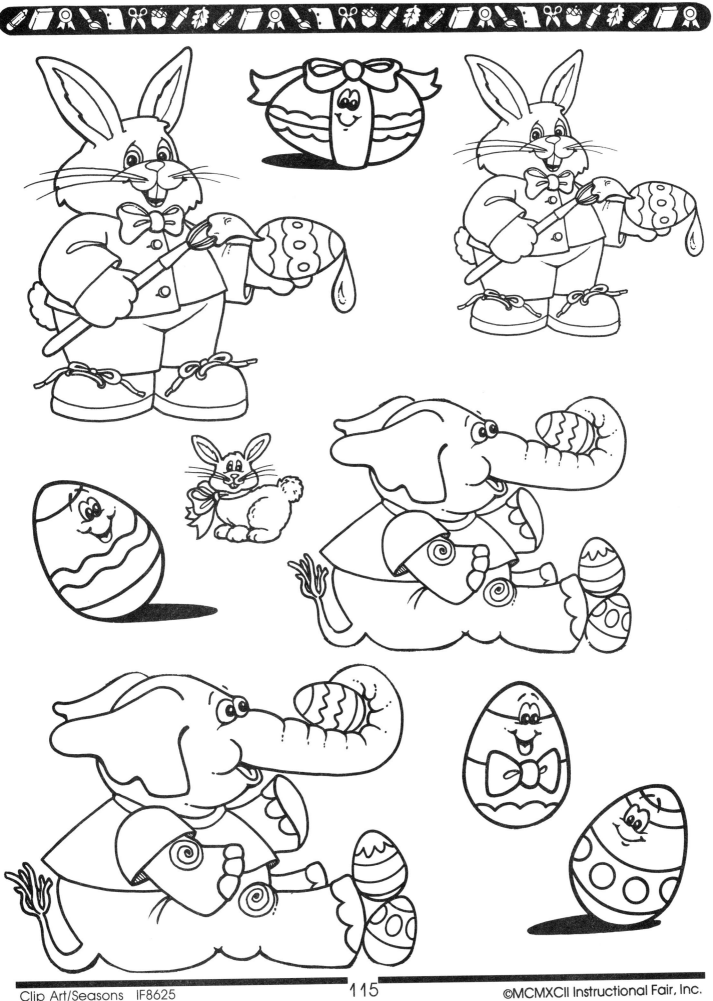

Clip Art/Seasons   IF8625

©MCMXCII Instructional Fair, Inc.

message: _____
_____
_____
_____
_____
_____

signed _____

date _____

SPRINGING FORWARD!

Clip Art/Seasons   IF8625

Clip Art/Seasons IF8625

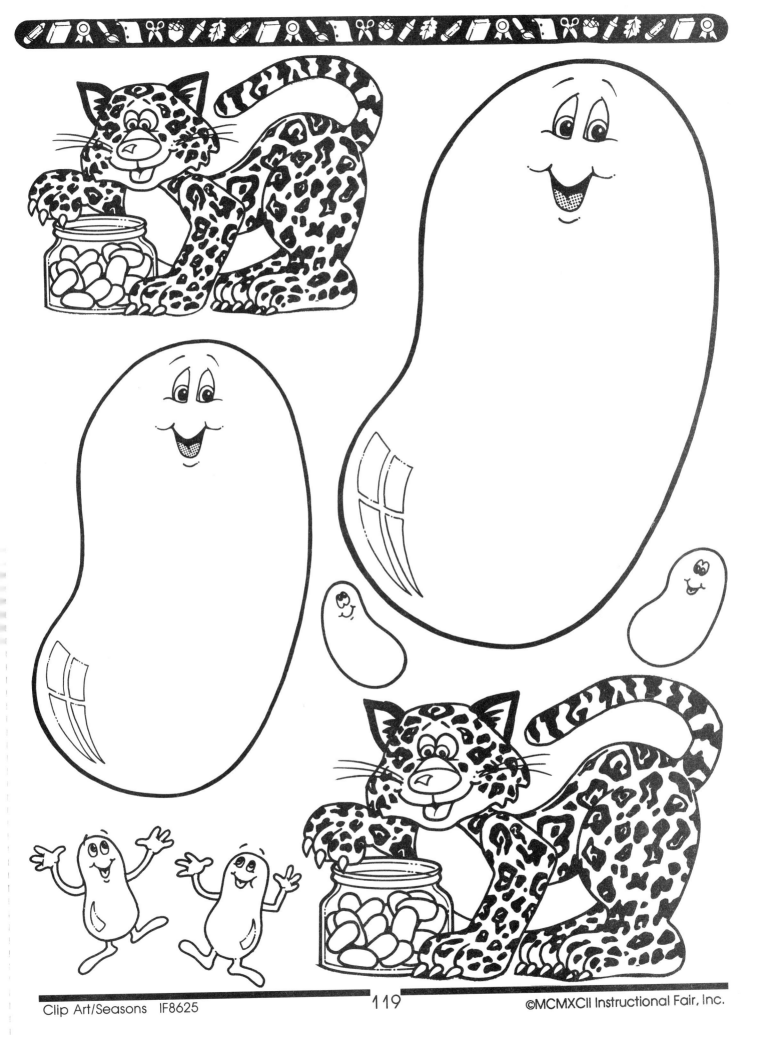

119

APRIL SHOWERS!

Clip Art/Seasons IF8625

"Bee" a Good Listener!

Something Sweet to Buzz About!

HOME SWEET HOME

HOME SWEET HOME

Name: _____

Date: _____

BzzZzzzzz

Clip Art/Seasons   IF8625

Clip Art/Seasons   IF8625   ©MCMXCII Instructional Fair, Inc.

MAY

MAYPOLE

_____'s
Name
GREEN THUMB AWARD!

Clip Art/Seasons   IF8625

name

plant

YELLOW

130

MEMORIAL DAY
May 30th

GREAT!

PRESENTED TO

FOR

PRESENTED THIS _____ DAY OF _____ 19 _____

SIGNATURE

Clip Art/Seasons   IF8625

Mother's Day

SUPER MOM

S U P E R

M O M

Dear Mom,

M _____
O _____
T _____
H _____
E _____
R _____

Love,

Clip Art/Seasons   IF8625

NATIONAL TRANSPORTATION WEEK

Clip Art/Seasons   IF8625

JUNE

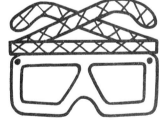

Your Work Is... Sun-sational!

It's Hot!

Name:

Date:

136

Father's Day

DYNAMIC DAD

DAD

DYNAMIC

Dear Dad,

F
_____

A
_____

T
_____

H
_____

E
_____

R
_____

Love,

She's a Grand Old Flag!

Flag Day — June 14

BETSY ROSS

YOUR PRIDE IS SHOWING!

Name _____

Date _____

JULY

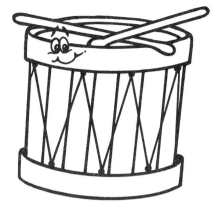

4th of July

STAR STUDENT

_____
name

SHINES IN

_____

Signed _____ Date _____

4th OF JULY

Clip Art/Seasons   IF8625

©MCMXCII Instructional Fair, Inc.

National
Clown Week

SUPER!

WOW!

PRESENTED TO

FOR

PRESENTED THIS _____ DAY OF _____ 19 ____

SIGNATURE

_____'s

name

batting _____ %

in _____

15

16

Clip Art/Seasons   IF8625
©MCMXCII Instructional Fair, Inc.

AUGUST

Clip Art/Seasons IF8625

Sweet Success!

Name _____

Date _____

Clip Art/Seasons   IF8625

©MCMXCII Instructional Fair, Inc.